What Do WHEELS AND CRANKS Do?

Heinemann
LIBRARY

David Glover

www.heinemann.co.uk/library
Visit our website to find out more information about Heinemann Library books.

To order:
☎ Phone 44 (0) 1865 888066
Send a fax to 44 (0) 1865 314091
 Visit the Heinemann Bookshop at www.heinemann.co.uk/library to browse our
🖥 catalogue and order online.

First published in Great Britain by Heinemann Library,
Halley Court, Jordan Hill, Oxford OX2 8EJ, part of
Harcourt Education. Heinemann is a registered
trademark of Harcourt Education Ltd.

Editorial: Clare Lewis and Katie Shepherd
Design: Victoria Bevan and Q2A Creative
Illustrations: Barry Atkinson (pp5, 17, 21), Douglas Hall
(p6) and Tony Kenyon (p4)
Picture Research: Mica Brancic
Production: Helen McCreath
Printed and bound in China by WKT Company
Limited

10 digit ISBN 0 431 06402 4
13 digit ISBN 978 0 431 06402 4
10 09 08 07 06
10 9 8 7 6 5 4 3 2 1

British Library Cataloguing in Publication Data
Glover, David
What do wheels and cranks do? - 2nd Edition
621.8'27
A full catalogue record for this book is available from
the British Library.

Acknowledgements
The publishers would like to thank the following for
permission to reproduce photographs: Trevor Clifford
pp1, 4, 5, 6, 7, 19top; Zefa pp8, 9, 11, 15bottom, 18;
Tony Stone Worldwide p10; Stockfile/Steven Behr
p12; Lori Adamski Peek/TSW p13; TRIP/R Drury p14/
G Horner p20; Quadrant Picture Library p15top;
Panos Pictures/ Ron Giling p16; Derek Cattani/Zefa
p17; Mary Evans Picture Library p19; Collections/
Brian Shuel p21.

Cover photograph reproduced with permission of
Getty Images.

The publishers would like to thank Angela Royston for
her assistance in the preparation of this book.

Every effort has been made to contact copyright
holders of any material reproduced in this book. Any
omissions will be rectified in subsequent printings if
notice is given to the publishers.

The paper used to print this book comes from
sustainable resources.

Any words appearing in the text in bold, **like this**, are
explained in the Glossary

Contents

What are wheels and cranks?

Everyone knows what a wheel is. It is one of the most important **inventions** ever made. Wheels are round and they turn to make things go. There are wheels on toys, bicycles, trains, cars, and lorries.

If no one had invented the wheel we would have to walk everywhere. We would need to carry things on our backs or drag them along the ground.

If you put a handle on one side of a wheel then you can use it to turn the wheel. This handle is called a crank. Sometimes a crank handle is just a bent bar.

crank handle

turn

You turn a crank handle to work this pencil sharpener.

Rollers

This girl is learning how to walk on a barrel. The barrel rolls along under her feet.

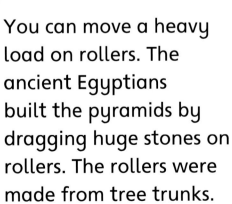

You can move a heavy load on rollers. The ancient Egyptians built the pyramids by dragging huge stones on rollers. The rollers were made from tree trunks.

You can do the same thing using pencils to move a book. When one pencil is uncovered behind as the book moves forwards, pick it up and move it to the front.

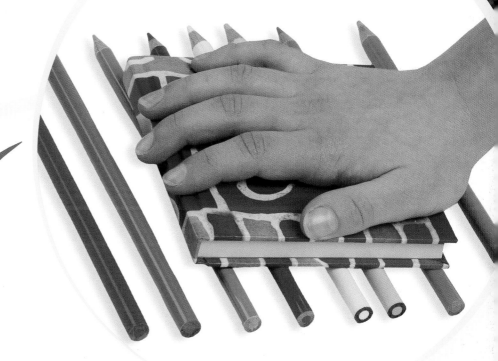

FACT FILE From rollers to wheels

Long ago, the use of rollers probably gave people the idea for the first wheels.

Cart and car wheels

The wheels on this old cart are made from wood. Wheels like this have been made for hundreds of years. A metal hoop is fixed around the wheel to stop it wearing away. These wheels give a very bumpy ride.

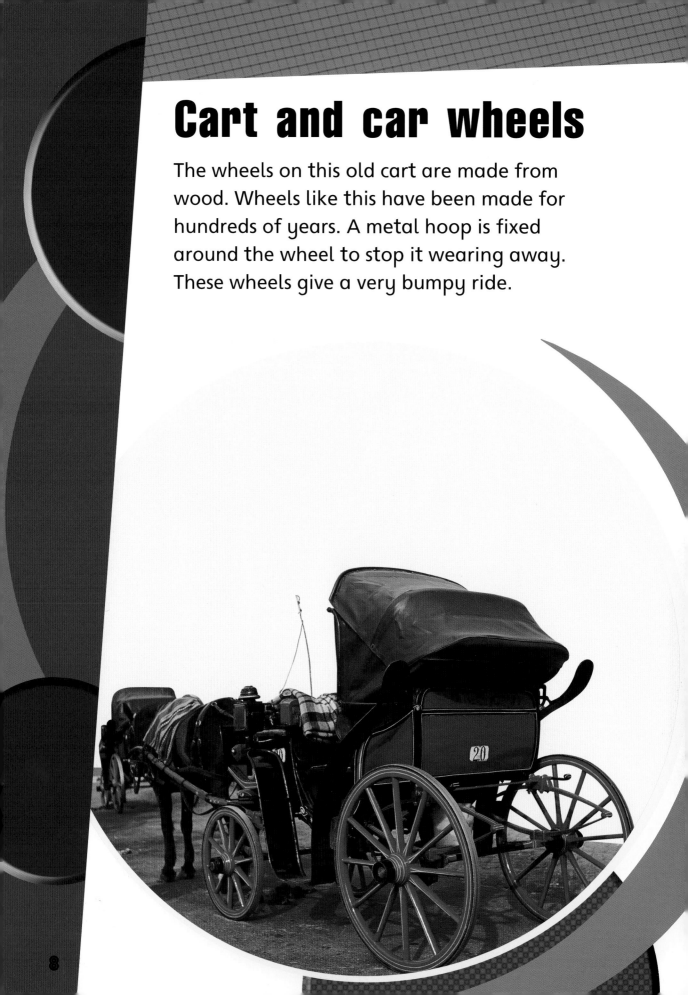

A modern car wheel has a thick rubber **tyre** wrapped around it. The tyre is filled with air, like a balloon. This helps the tyre to bounce over bumps on the road.

The pattern that is cut into a tyre is called the **tread**. The tread helps the tyre to **grip** on wet roads.

FACT FILE **Who invented the wheel?**

No one knows who invented the wheel. People may have invented wheels in different parts of the world at different times. Carts with wheels were made in ancient Egypt more than 5,000 years ago.

Bicycle wheels

A racing bicycle has very light-weight wheels. Thin wire **spokes** hold the **rim** of the wheel in place. Wheels like these are good for riding fast on smooth road surfaces.

A mountain bike has much thicker wheels than a racing bike. They are heavier and make the bike slower, but they are stronger. Wheels like these are good for riding over rough ground.

FACT FILE **A smooth ride**

Big wheels give a smoother ride than small wheels. Imagine a bicycle with tiny roller-skate wheels. It would soon make you saddle sore!

Boards and blades

A skateboard has two pairs of small rubber wheels. Each wheel spins round on a **rod**. This rod is called an **axle**. Inside the wheels are small metal balls called **ball bearings**. They make the wheels turn smoothly.

These roller blades have four hard plastic wheels in a row. The **stiff** boots help you to balance. They stop you from twisting your ankles. An expert roller blader can go as fast as a person on a bicycle.

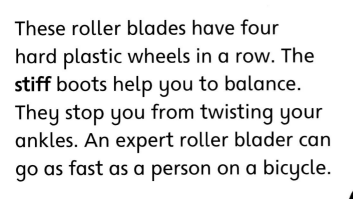

FACT FILE Skating tip

Skateboards and roller blades go best on a smooth hard ground. Their small wheels do not work well on grass or mud.

Tractor and truck wheels

Tractor wheels have big tyres to stop them sinking in soft mud. The deep **tread** on the tyres gives extra **grip** when the ground is slippery.

This truck can go almost anywhere on its huge wheels. It can drive through deep water and climb steep hills. It can even drive over other trucks!

FACT FILE Giant trucks

The biggest tyres in the world are twice as tall as a man. They are fitted to giant dumper trucks.

Crank handles

This machine is used for crushing sugar cane to squeeze out the juice. The mules are turning the crank handle as they walk around. This makes the rollers turn and crush the cane.

There is a crank handle on this old car. You turn the handle to get the engine going. Modern cars have a separate starter **motor** that works when you turn a key.

crank handle

FACT FILE Records and movies

crank handle

crank handle

The first record players and the first movie cameras had crank handles to make them work. Modern machines use electric motors to make them turn.

Pedal power

This woman turns her spinning wheel by pedalling with her foot. The pedal pushes a crank to make the wheel turn round.

Cranks make pedal cars go. First you push one pedal, then the other. Your pushes turn the crank, and the crank turns the car's wheels.

FACT FILE **Cranky cycles**

The very first bicycles were worked by cranks. The cyclist pushed the pedal down to make the wheels turn.

Crank it up!

A canal **lock** is worked by a crank handle. The lock keeper turns the handle to let water in or out of the lock. The handle opens a hole in the lock gate to let the water through.

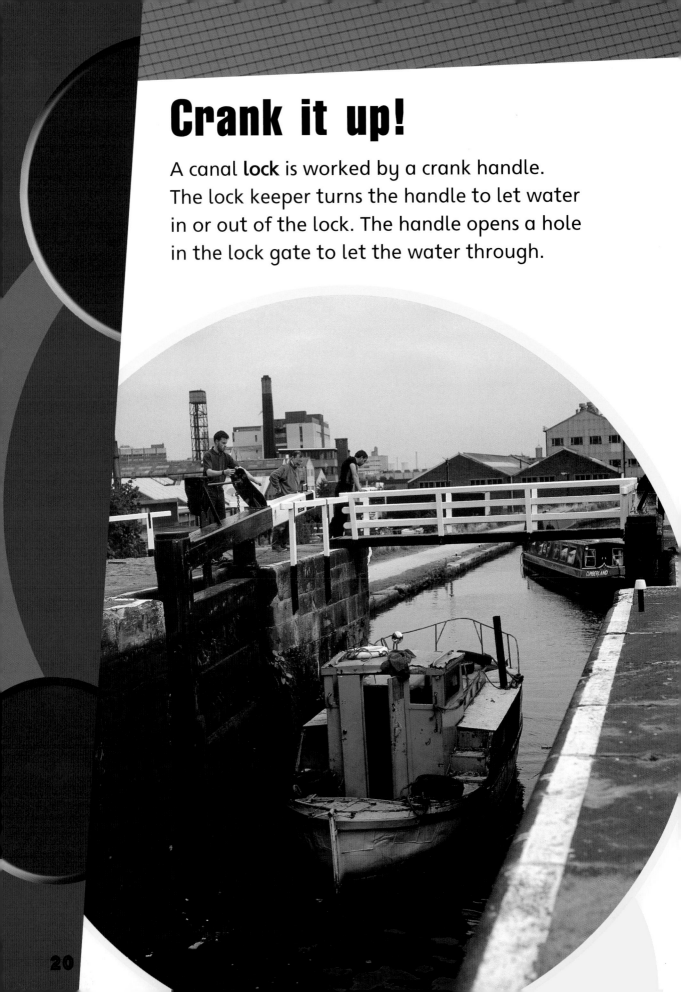

An organ grinder turns a crank handle to make music. His organ plays tunes as he winds the handle. The quicker he turns the handle, the faster the music plays.

FACT FILE **Winding up**

The handle on a water well is a crank. It winds up the rope to lift the bucket.

crank handle

Activities

Test the power of wheels

1. You will need a toy truck or skateboard.
2. Tie a piece of thread or string around a heavy book.
3. Pull the book along the floor.

4. Now put the book on top of the truck or skateboard and pull it again.
5. Do the wheels make it easier to pull the book?

Using a crank handle

1. You will need an egg whisk like the one in the photo.
2. Use your fingers to turn the big wheel that turns the beaters.

3. Now use the handle to turn the wheel.
4. Which way is easier? The handle of the whisk is a crank.

Glossary

axle   the rod or bar in the middle of a wheel

ball bearings   small metal balls inside a wheel which make it turn smoothly

grip   hold tightly

inventions   ideas for new machines that no one has made before.

lock   invention that stops you opening a door or a lid unless you have a special key

motor   machine that uses electricity or fuels such as petrol or coal to make things move

rim   the outside part or edge of a wheel

rod   bar or stick, often made from metal

saddle sore   feeling uncomfortable after sitting on a hard seat or saddle for too long!

spokes   metal wires that hold the rim of a bicycle wheel in place

stiff   difficult to bend

tread   the pattern in a rubber tyre that helps it grip the road when it is wet or muddy

tyre   the rubber ring put around the rim of a wheel

Index